CRACKS

Unapologetic Essays on Growing Up and Getting Gay

CRACKS

Unapologetic Essays on
Growing Up and Getting Gay

MELISSA SHER

Girl & Dog
PUBLISHING

PORTLAND, OREGON

CRACKS:

UNAPOLOGETIC ESSAYS ON GROWING UP AND GETTING GAY

ISBN-13: 978-0-578-64332-8

Published by Girl and Dog Publishing
Portland, OR

Printed in the United States of America
First Edition February 2020

Cover Design by Make Your Mark Publishing Solutions
Interior Layout by Make Your Mark Publishing Solutions
Editing by Make Your Mark Publishing Solutions

Drawings by Melissa Sher

CONTENTS

ACKNOWLEDGEMENTS

I t takes a whole lot of people to raise a human and a whole lot of people to turn that human's life into a book.

To those who raised me: Mom and Dad, thank you for making reading such an important thing in my life. Thank you also for letting me be me as a kid and keeping my hair short so a lot of these stories could exist today. Love you both. Emily J., thank you for cueing me into the "butthead" I really am and honestly putting my life on a path I never would have explored. Naime, thank you for being the kindest friend during the weirdest times. Kimberly, I could not have done any of the last six years without you. Thank you for the space and support in my writing. And Kat, thank you for taking that shot of Fireball and never not hanging around me since. Your encouragement while I wrote this book has been the thing that kept me doing it.

To those who helped with the book: Mr. Pierson, thank you for being the English teacher who made me love writing. Thank you, Kelly Cutchin for basically being my therapist and forcing me to figure out what I was actually trying to say in all of these essays. You're the best writing coach that exists. Thank you, Monique D. Mensah for making my dreams come true and turning a lot of years of writing into a thing I can hold and read. The work you do and the patience you have while doing it is inspiring.

To those still figuring things out: Thank you for being you, no matter who you are. It is the most freeing and important thing you can do for yourself and also for those who you might not even know are looking to you as an example.

DEDICATION

For Desi. Be you no matter what they tell you.

POP

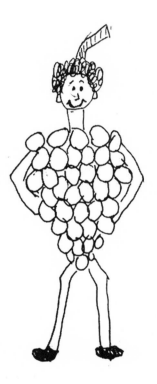

There are two types of people: those who hate Halloween and those who have costume bins they talk about all the time. I have zero costumes, probably because costumes are expensive and take up space. During my twenties, my living arrangements were:

1. A rented room in a house
2. A 1960s truck camper (shared with someone)
3. The left side of a friend's couch (shared with a cat)
4. A basement

My jobs were:
1. A personal trainer
2. A waitress at a gluten-free fish house (their slogan: If it smells like fish, eat it)
3. A rafting guide
4. A bicycling guide
5-123. More serving positions

There you have it—a picture of success. So unless I wanted to purchase costumes with the quarters found under my portion of the couch, I wouldn't be "fun" at Halloween for some time.

When I was trying to date men circa 2010, I met a guy named Vince, and he asked me to a party that October 31. I hear the name "Vince," and I picture a man not quite tall enough, who knows he's not quite tall enough and has an attitude to compensate for what he lacks in inches (likely everywhere). He might own a leather vest and definitely wears shirts that exclusively let the top inch of his chest hair billow from the collar. Gross. I didn't have a hard and fast rule about not dating Vinces, but I should have. That said, I wasn't the type of gal who was inundated with dating propositions, so I accepted his invitation.

As stated previously, I had no costumes and, as a rule, anyone who goes to a Halloween party as an adult sans alternate identity is a L.O.S.E.R. Too poor for costume purchase, I threw on a cowboy hat my roommate had, a men's oversized button down plaid shirt that I'd gotten at the Goodwill and wore on rafting trips (work uniform), and jean shorts, which stopped at a respectful one inch above the knee, that I wore on the daily. If it's not already, it should be made clear that this was not a "hot cowgirl" costume. This was more like if the hot cowgirl had a creepy, sad uncle—This would be what he wore. Nevertheless, I persisted.

I made my way to Vince's house, and when he opened the door, his reaction to me and/or my costume was, "Oh." He chuckled and followed it up with, "You look like a fucking dyke." This was our first date, and that was literally his first sentence to me. I don't remember my response, but I do remember not turning around and walking the heck out, which would have been the only appropriate one. Instead, I went into his apartment and waited for him to get ready.

Shockingly, nothing amounted to the night with Vince. It ended rather abruptly when I found out he was over ten years my senior (gag). Just as well for him, the party was rife with slutty nurse costumes way less "dykish" than my cowgirl. I went home to sleep before ten— We both won.

Rewind ten Halloweens.

Upon entering adolescence, "bad" features are worn like scarlet letters, seeming, to us, to be the only thing the rest of the world sees. I remember puberty not as a slow, forgiving process but as waking up one morning suddenly not a kid anymore. At this time, masking ourselves becomes popularized. What we looked like in our minds was what we thought we were worth as a people. Our zits were covered with foundation that made them worse, our body odor disguised with arguably more horrible-smelling deodorant or cologne (Axe if you're a kid of the '90s), and our bodies cloaked in whatever clothing trends were in style. In a way, this constant covering-up charade likely formed a belief from a young age that, because our raw selves might be a little too much for the general public, measures should be taken to alter who we really are.

I was, let's just say, *unfortunate looking* when my twelfth birthday came around. My nose decided to be the only element of my body not held back in growth by the gymnastics I did in childhood. It flourished like the first flowers of spring, leaving my face behind without so much as a goodbye. Long hair may not only have made my gender more apparent but may also have drawn some attention away from the mountain in the middle of my face. But no ... Mom thought my hair was "just adorable," so that was enough to make it stay. Lastly came the braces, acne, and new school respectively.

Seventh grade was weird. I looked like (see above), had few social skills and even fewer friends. Looking back, I should have stopped taking advice from Mom at that age. The hair was a bad idea, the braces were a bad idea, and I'm going to go ahead and take this time to blame her for the genetics causing the Mount Malfunction that was growing on my face without signs of stopping. So why would I seek her help for a Halloween costume?

Mom is a crafty lady and has always prided herself in that. She loves a theme. Afternoons could be spent all day at Michaels pouring over the stamps and various types of adhesives. This is why I assume I went to her when I needed a costume for the seventh and eighth grade Halloween dance, my first school dance. It was as if Mom had been waiting her entire life for me to come to her with a solution to a costume needing to be debuted. She knew way too soon, and with seemingly little thought, exactly what I was going to be and how I was going to be it. The costume she chose for me could have been used at any point in my life: during trick or treating with my neighbors at age six, during elementary school, when I was five … Basically, it would have been fine at any other previous juncture.

"You should be a bunch of grapes!" she said.

I blame myself for not objecting. I will forever blame myself for that.

The problem quickly became not the costume itself, but how it was planned to be rendered.

"Melissa, come here and put this sweatshirt on." Mom handed me a purple Fruit of the Loom and went to the other room.

"Now, start blowing these up," she said as she came back in with a bag of purple water balloons.

"Are you sure balloons are a good idea? Can't we use paper cutouts or something?" I said, slowly putting together the pieces of what was happening.

"Yes! Balloons will look real. Now make some bigger and some smaller so it looks like a real bunch."

As I blew up balloons, Mom attached each tied-off end to a safety pin. Most of the inflated purple balls were to be pinned around the collar. With this setup, not even a glass of water was making it close to my lips. The rows continued down my body, creating a V, tapering down to the last bushel of barely inflated balloons, which fell right over my crotch. If Frida Khalo took to painting her bottom half, this would be a nice abstract representation

11

of what might have been going on. This was not the end. A "stem" hat (twisted brown grocery bag) was then placed on top of my head. Once secured to my nearly non-existent hair, I was deemed ready.

At the dance, I stood in the corner, the darkest spot in the room, cursing with my eyes the cats, princesses, superheroes, and kids *too cool* (when you're in junior high, no costume = cool) to even wear a costume.

Then it happened.

A boy started making his way over to my corner. I was horrified. Was this a joke? Was he coming over to mock me? Who was putting him up to this? I had no physical option but to keep looking straight at him as he approached because of the neck brace of large balloons attached to my collar.

"Would you like to dance?"

Shock filled the room. This would be my first slow dance with a boy. Not thinking that, given my costume, logistics would have to be taken into consideration for the activity, I murmured a barely audible, "Okay."

We made our way to the floor. At this stage of life, slow dancing involved the girl's hands on the shoulders of the boy, sufficient one-and-a-half-foot gap between midsections, and the boy's hands on the girl's hips.

Issues:

1. I couldn't raise my hands as high as his shoulders.

2. My hips were balloons.
3. The balloons hit his stomach, creating static friction on his shirt as we moved.

We "danced" awkwardly, editing the normal dance position to accommodate my new circumference. My hands had to be placed on his hips, his on my shoulders. This reconfiguration did nothing to help ease any pending suspicions in the case of my gender.

We remained like this for however long a 98 Degrees song takes to be over, making small steps from side to side and calling it dancing.

All of a sudden ...

POP!

The friction of the balloons' back and forth against his shirt caused an explosion.

We stopped. An experience no thirteen-year-old should go through is part of her person effectively blowing up while at her first school dance during her first slow song. Like the pop, everything in my head was loud, then all of a sudden, it was silent—maybe just to me or maybe in the room; I can't recall. The middle balloon sounded, and we removed our hands, now just standing there facing one another, neither knowing how to proceed. Luckily, the final chorus of the song began to fade. The music changed pace from the soothing melody to a fast Backstreet Boys tune, freeing everyone's hands from one another's bodies and bringing them into the air above their heads, relinquishing us from any further commitment to slow dancing. I considered this to be a singular stroke of luck for me that year.

"I have to go to the bathroom," I said and ran from the dance floor as fast as the grapes would allow. I made my way out of the school multi-purpose room, not knowing what I would do once there. Mid-journey, I noticed my friend Cindy had just arrived. She, too, was a bunch of grapes for Halloween. Hers, however, were not made from balloons, but from purple felt cut into ovals, stuffed just a little and sewn to another felt oval. Nice, soft, figure-forgiving felt. I watched Cindy dance with ease on the floor, moving her arms in any direction she pleased, unrestricted by balloons. Then I turned in a huff and left.

That year in middle school, my costume rejected me. Perhaps it set me up to handle Future Vince rejecting my costume. Halloween should be the one time of year when you can be whatever or whomever you want: Batman, Miss America, an Olympian, a cat; the choice is yours. I wanted to feel comfortable like Cindy did at the dance. Instead, my grapes just enhanced the new person I felt like I was—awkward, self-conscious, and unable to do much but stand in the corner.

I spent a while being straight. To be clear, I spent about twenty-seven years in that costume. I went on dates with guys named Vince. And that one year for Halloween, when I showed up at his door, he thought it was a costume, but little did he or even I know that I'd picked from my daily life the most comforting clothes I had to put on that night. Perhaps I was unknowingly dressed up as my future self, the self I would discover in a few years.

Vince, if you're reading this, which you most definitely are not, I guess I am now what *you* would call a "dyke." I won't give you the credit for figuring it out before I did, but maybe you did help me realize why I don't like Halloween—It's just another day to dress up as something we are not, and I'm kind of tired of that.

STRIP CLUBS

B y November of 2008, I had made only three friends since moving from the Midwest to Portland, Oregon a few months prior. My housemates, Beth and Emily, were two of the three, and the third was a woman from work. As a card-carrying introvert, I literally had not met anyone outside of the necessary walls within my day-to-day life.

Standing in our kitchen one afternoon, Beth piped up, "My parents are in town, and we're going to get dinner. You want to come?"

Another day, and I might have politely declined, but this day was my twenty-third birthday *and* election day, when it would be decided if Barack Obama would be our new president. Unable to justify solitude on this night, I agreed.

We dined at an Indian restaurant where there was nothing to be heard in the entire place, save for the low murmur of televisions broadcasting the election results as they came in. The final tally was moments away as we sat on the edge of our seats with chapati in hand, spicy food in our mouths, and hope in our hearts.

As the server presented the bill, Beth's parents reached to grab it, but it was soon forgotten as the election results came in. The broadcaster said, *"This is a moment so many people have waited for—Senator Barack Obama is projected to be the next president of the United States!"*

A collective sigh of relief seemed to come over the whole room. It was quickly apparent that the patrons, the staff, and our table were all on the same team. "*Yes we can!*" sounded from the TVs as if from our mascot after winning the big game. Everyone turned to the tables around them. We shook hands with our dining neighbors while "*Yes we can*" was repeated by the crowds on the news. Everyone's eyes that previously held doubt were now shimmering with the hope that maybe *we could*.

Once the hair on our arms calmed, the four of us left the restaurant with a bit of a kick in our step.

"Well, it's time for us to turn in," Beth's parents told us.

I concurred and was ready to use their departure as my cue to say I'd be heading home as well just as Beth turned to me. "Hey, wanna meet up with some of my friends at a bar?"

An often misunderstood quality we introverts possess is that plans must be known in advance. Who, what, when, where and why are key facts we *need*, preferably forty-eight hours beforehand minimum, for us to mentally prepare for any situation. But as the new kid in town, the possibility of friends was too great to turn down. I wasn't making much of an effort to meet people on my own. Truth be told, I didn't really know how to go about it as an adult who wasn't in school surrounded by a smorgasbord of friendship potential day in and out. Here, it seemed I'd be a fool to turn down Beth doing the dirty work for me. So, even though all I wanted to do was put on my house-only gray sweat suit, I replied for the second time that evening, though a bit more hesitantly, "Yeah, I'd love to."

Sensing my possible regret, Beth assured me, "Great! They just want to meet up for a quick drink before celebrating the elections somewhere else."

Great! I thought. The only thing worse to an introvert than going out is going out to multiple locations.

"Somewhere else" turned out to be a brick building spray painted black and windowless. Flashing lights surrounded a hot pink neon sign that read, "Sassy's." I'd heard about this place before. An intimidatingly large man sat by the door. We were at a strip club. Sassy's was like a right of passage to newcomers in Portland, a city that boasted most strip clubs per capita. It was known as the "classy" club. Rumor was people had business meetings at their chicken strip (pun probably intended) lunch buffet, which, apparently, Sassy's was also known for. Frankly, the combination of business, chicken, and titties was not one I drove 2,000 miles to take part in, but here we were.

In addition to introversion, cheapness due to poorness was another winning quality I claimed. That night, I was donned in clothes my mom bought for me back in high school: jeans and a green cable knit turtleneck sweater paired with a smart brown corduroy peacoat from the Gap.

Severely concerned about my attire, I reached out and touched Beth's sleeve. "Say, this isn't *just* a bar ..." I said, hoping to point out her error in location.

Beth and I fumbled in our pockets and handed our IDs to the bouncer. As he handed Beth's ID back to her, she turned to reassure me. "Like I said, we are just going in for a second to meet up with a few of my friends, then we'll go to a different bar."

Before I could argue, she was inside the black building, and I felt I had no choice but to follow. What was I to do, be the girl in the turtleneck sweater who wouldn't go into a strip club?

Once inside, I sauntered up to the bar as my first order of business. As I did this, I tried not to touch a thing. It was too dark to measure any level of cleanliness in the establishment, and while I'm not generally a stickler for such things, when there are naked people about, I have more concern.

I walked up to the bar like I was a regular, peered down to the lowest shelf and ordered a vodka soda. I drank my poor man's, college girl cocktail like a shot. As I tilted the glass upward to let the ice—likely holding on to some last alcoholic moisture—cascade into my mouth, I saw in my peripheral vision where Beth and her friends were seated. They were perched on stools right up against the stage.

Beth waved, and I saw her mouth, "Over here!" as she pointed down at an open stool apparently for me. The three men with her, whom I assumed were her friends, occupied the seats next to mine. I wanted nothing to do with any of them. I wanted to take my introverted self home and go to bed. It was nearing ten p.m. after all. But instead, I ordered another drink and made my way over to my stool. Maneuvering through a crowded bar is often tricky, but add lap dances and the task of evading men in curiously baggy pants, and you have yourself a downright challenge.

I arrived at the stage, removed my peacoat to cover the leather seat of the stool, sat on top of it, and silently vowed that burning the coat would be the first thing I did if I made it out of there alive.

I glanced over at Beth and noticed she looked completely at ease leaning against the stage, peering up at the strippers as if every bar she had ever been to had naked women dancing for dollars in front of her.

I had not yet looked at the stage once.

At this point in my life, I was what they call a "never nude." I was not comfortable with nudity—mine or anyone else's. If it wasn't totally weird to shower in a bathing suit, I would have. Later in life, I would realize this was actually a strong aversion to the male body, but I didn't know this at the time. So I closed my eyes—an odd thing to do in the front row of a strip club—and told myself I had to do this; I had to look up. And I did. And what I saw was amazing.

The stage was small with two poles set concerningly close to the stools where we patrons sat. The women on the poles were holding themselves parallel to the ground, seemingly floating. Lights came down from the ceiling, hitting their bodies, accenting their muscles and reflecting off their sweat. Each stripper wore something different, playing to her specific personality. One woman was covered in tattoos, appearing to actually be clothed. Another wore the cliché of pink knee-high socks, impossibly high lucite heels, and pink bows tied in her platinum blonde hair. These were athletes of the strangest kind, and I stared, completely fascinated. They were pulling moves on that pole that most Olympians, save for the gymnasts, could not imagine doing. I watched, mesmerized as their skin seemed to struggle to the point just before ripping to encase their bulging muscles.

My admiration did not go unnoticed, and soon, one of the strippers came forward in a way that no one had ever moved toward me in my life. My biggest fear, that I didn't even know I had until that moment, was realized: A stripper was talking to me. Without hesitation, she knelt in front of me, knees pointing to either side of the room, rolled her hips back and whispered, "What are you doing here tonight?"

A naked stranger was talking to an introverted, midwestern twenty-three-year-old never nude cloaked in a turtleneck sweater, seated upon a peacoat. I wondered what she might do next. I wondered if I was as much of an anomaly to her as she was to me.

In any stage performance it is understood that the ones above us on the stage hold a talent that we commoners below in the seats do not; there is an underlying respect for the performers. When stripping is involved, people replace respect with shame. They suddenly think, in their seats, they are better than the sad girls on stage. A drip of respect melts from us with each piece of clothing shed, replaced with a building sense of power. I didn't know why, but I knew I felt the opposite toward them. I admired in the strippers everything I lacked in myself. I would never expose as much of myself to anyone, internally or externally.

What are you doing here tonight? She had probably asked this very question to a million men before, each simple enough to truly believe that when a stripper inquired about his evening plans, she actually wanted to know. He might surmise that maybe she really was attracted to him, and he wouldn't go home alone *again*. Maybe this time, she would grace his disgusting bed in the flesh and not just as replayed images in his mind.

I wanted to give her something original, something other than "celebrating my birthday." I wanted her to know I was different than the rest of the people in this bar and I would never actually choose to celebrate another year of life in this way. I think, after an uncomfortable amount of silence, Beth answered (something I didn't hear) on my behalf, but that did not satiate the stripper's need to embarrass me.

The stripper prodded as I sat frozen on my stool, consciously trying to look only at her face. Staring into her eyes, I was surprised to not find sadness behind them as I assumed, like everyone else, came with the profession. Instead, they squinted at me, mocking me until she persisted, "What are *you* doing here tonight?"

I looked around the stage at the other people watching her, *staring* at her naked body as though it was *owed* to them, which is no less than what one is supposed to do at a strip club, I guess. While they stared in a way their parents taught them is rude, I continued staring in a strange sort of admiration. In any event, she was still waiting in a very deep squat for that answer.

I repeated her question to buy time. "What am I doing here tonight?"

She placed one hand on the ground in front of her and leaned in closer. "Yeah, what are you doing tonight?" she whispered.

I had nothing.

If you had told me prior to this night that some-one asking about your evening's plans could be sexy, I wouldn't have believed you. But she said this in a more seductive way than anyone had ever spoken to me up to that point.

I looked at her, pleading with my stare to go away, hoping my expression could say what I couldn't: *Look lady, I respect you. Move on to that guy with the boner to my right.*

Instead, I cleared my throat. "Celebrating Obama's win," I said. Of course, I was. Of course, I in my turtle-neck, I with my ass that feared the touch of a strip club's leather seat beneath it, and I who wanted nothing more than the stripper to think I was a good person, was, of course, there "celebrating Obama's win."

"I bet you are." She smiled, looking down at *all* of us from the stage, having gotten exactly what she wanted.

Beth and I soon left. We had broken the unwritten rule that you can't sit in the front row without letting a dollar break free from your wallet and into the stripper's boot or string. With as many ones as we had entered with, we walked down the street. The hair on my arms raised for a second time that night. I thought about those strippers on the poles and the difference between them and me. I went into Sassy's that night afraid to even touch the bar stools and thinking the strippers needed my compassion, my awareness of what I thought their situation was. I left realizing I had learned from them something I might not fully understand for a while. I learned that some of us just speculate in our turtlenecks, covering as many inches as possible, unable to reveal anything, even to ourselves. Others say, "Fuck it," grab the pole by their feet, and render us speechless.

THE FRIEND TRACK

woke up on September 2, 2008 in an empty room, save for a borrowed piece of foam about the size of a twin mattress. Four months prior, I had graduated from the University of Kansas then spent the summer managing a coffee shop to save money so I could get the heck out of the Midwest. I had worked at the shop since my sophomore year, so I asked some regular customers, people who knew me well at that point, what they thought my next move should be. I knew I needed to go somewhere; wheat blowing in the wind had all but lost its initial charm and, I swear, if I heard one more girl swooning over Tim McGraw at a stoplight as she applied makeup to her hungover face, I knew I would just stop living. After graduation, I proudly possessed a bachelor of fine arts degree that I intended to do nothing with, proving I made bad decisions for myself. I reasoned that perhaps the people who had positioned themselves in such a way where five-dollar lattes every morning was manageable might have better ideas for my success. They did not.

One guy told me, "Join the Army! It'll be good for you."

Mary, my favorite customer, said, "Move to California; it'll force you to make money!"

Dan, my least favorite, came in hot with the advice. "Maybe you should have gone to business school in the first place." Duh, *Dan*.

I decided on Portland, Oregon for no reason other than it was on the West Coast. The East Coast evoked a cold feeling to me both in weather and atmosphere, maybe because the ivy leagues are there; I don't know. In the end, I chose Oregon because it's cheaper than California. And that's roughly the uninteresting story of how I found myself positioned on a rectangle of foam in my freshly rented room in a large, old house with four new housemates found on Craigslist.

I stared up at the ceiling for probably an hour before I sat up and said out loud to myself, "What the fuck am I doing?" I was alone in a new part of the country with no friends, no money, and no job. I dropped my head back down onto my pillow. With nowhere to go and no one to see, what was the pressing need to get up anyway?

Outside of childhood, making friends is a downright task. During our school years, we see the same people every day. We have time to find each other's quirks endearing and form friendships rooted in many years of shared experiences. Share a toy sailboat in the sandbox with a kid in kindergarten one day, offer the crusts off your PB&J the next, and *BAM!* No matter if they have a lazy eye and snot, impossibly green and textured, coming out of their noses, a gorgeous friendship is formed. Conversely, in adulthood, we generally only have brief encounters at a coffee shop or in line at the grocery. Thanks to herpes, sharing snacks is no longer socially acceptable, so initial reactions and snap judgments from a quick scan of clothing, demeanor, and number of piercings are all we have to go on. First impressions can either leave us running in the other direction or find us sticking around to incite a conversation. A shame, really. I often think about how many people I have deemed *not for me* in adult life solely due to their nasal septum piercing.

I realized a couple of years into my art degree that I had no real interest in pursuing the arts professionally, but I had even less interest in staying in Kansas one hour longer than I had to. So rather than switch majors, I stuck it out and walked the stage to collect my very expensive and very meaningless degree. It promptly served as a bookmark in a used personal training book I got for fifty dollars, thus beginning my new career at a gym. After moving west and taking the exam to become certified as a trainer, I landed a position in a local athletic club. Even though I surmised my new friends would be a bunch of no-necked meatheads, I was excited to have somewhere to go other than the piece of foam. As it turned out, most of the other trainers had necks but were married and/or not really in the market for new friends. It was one of those *we got along at work but would not be going for boiled chicken and broccoli any time soon* kind of situations.

After a few more weeks in my new city and uncertain why I wasn't yet thriving, I lay on the foam again one morning thinking of ways to make friends. It was 2008, and online dating was on the verge of becoming popularized. Trouble was I wasn't looking for a mate so much as a friend I could count on being in my life for more than a few weeks. I googled "Meetups in Portland" and came across quite a few running groups. Running was an activity I loved, mostly because I could do it alone. These, however, were desperate times and desperate measures—talking to strangers—would need to be taken.

I found a running group called The Red Lizards that met at a track within walking distance from my house every Tuesday. I had seen people in town with t-shirts bearing the group's name on the back, so I figured there would be a good number of people from which I could hand pick some new friends. Plus, belonging to something sounded nice. On the walk over to the track for my first workout, I saw a guy walking a few steps ahead of me wearing a shirt with a red lizard on the back. Thinking surprisingly little about it, I hastened my step until I was next to him, mustered all the confidence I had acquired in my entire life as an introvert, and said to this stranger, "Oh, are you going to the track workout, too?"

He looked over at me, surprised by his sudden companion, and said, "Yes, I go with my girlfriend every week." Then he looked back toward the road ahead.

When a person immediately pulls the *significant other* card, it can mean one of a couple things.

1. They are arrogant. Whether they actually have a significant other or not, they automatically assume, without a shred of doubt, you are hitting on them.

2. They have a significant other but not a significant life. They are the type of person that, when talking about anything they do, they say, "*We* like this" or "*We* aspire to …" They don't have an independent bone in their codependent body.

Awesome, I thought. *Newsflash, man, I'm not hitting on you; I just want some damn friends.* I let my pace fall back and pressed on with shame as my only companion.

Once I arrived at the track, I made it a point to avoid the man with his case of significant otherness. People were milling around. The group was small, and this made it easy and imperative to strike up other conversations. One may not notice someone in a group of fifty standing in the corner creepily making eyes at people, but someone in a group of eight with the same behavior will surely be suspect.

With this reasoning, I wasted no time starting in on a runner's lunge to look busy.

I heard a woman's voice from behind me as I was deep in a hip flexor stretch. "Are you new to this group?"

I turned to see a woman around my age. "Yeah. How about you?" I said, trying to be cool, keeping everything within me from screaming, *Yes, will you be my friend please?*

"Me, too," she said while assuming a stretch next to me. "I'm a little nervous about this workout. I'm not very fast," she continued casually and, as women do, throwing in a self-deprecating comment for no reason at all.

I, of course, took it to mean she wanted to be my friend immediately. I started picturing things we might do: movies, hikes I'd wanted to go on with someone; we could cook stuff . . . In my head, a beautiful friendship was born after two spoken sentences and not even knowing one another's name.

Rather than start in with my plans for her, I assured her, "I wouldn't worry about it; I'm not that fast either." I lied. I was actually pretty fast when it came to track. I carried the nickname "Quadzilla" throughout my young adult life due to the large circumference of my thighs, which were not unlike medium-sized tree trunks. This served me well, powering me through my high school track and field days.

Nonetheless, we started the workout together. Conversation happened naturally—the standard "What do you do? How long have you lived here?" talk. My first best friend in Portland! Now, I had to get down to the business of convincing her that she wanted the same thing. A small glitch in the plans occurred. She was right—She was not that fast, and as much as I wanted to be friends, I could not, in good conscience, continue at her snail's pace. I ditched her for the rest of the run by reasoning we could catch up after.

The workout started nearing a close, and I realized I had to act fast if I wanted to leave with a friend. I went back to the group to find her.

Once I recognized the back of her head, I said, "So, I never got your name."

She turned to face me, "I'm Julie. Hope you enjoyed this group. Seems like a great way to meet people."

Assuming she would never have said that to me if she didn't want to be my new friend, I boldly responded, "I'm Melissa"—Insert slightly too long of a pause— "So, if you ever want to run outside the group, let me know! I'm always looking for running partners." I lied again. I was nervous, actually perspiring from the conversation. And I *needed* her. I also became very aware that it sounded like I was asking her on a date.

"Yeah, that would be fun."

She said yes. Yes! My excitement was greater than if I *had* just actually been asked on a date. I was filled with sudden relief at her response and ready to leave. As I gathered my things, I realized I had no way of contacting her, and we had made no official plans.

She had begun to walk away, but I didn't let that stop me, "Hey!" I called too loudly. She turned back around. Not waiting for her to be within a socially appropriate distance, I, still shouting, said, "Um, so can I give you my phone number, and if you have time this week, we could go for that run or something?" *Good move*, I thought. *Put the ball in her court.* I was slightly paranoid that she was beginning to just appease me.

"Oh," she started in a high-pitched voice, stalling. Then, "I don't have my phone or a pen. Maybe I'll just see you here next week?" She said this casually, with little concern that we might never see each other again. Soon, I was watching her walk away from me once more.

Here it was. There is always a moment when desperation starts to become apparent. When various mechanisms in a person's brain should send a warning signal that enough has been said. That the conversation is done. When she began to walk away is when I, too, should have walked away.

Instead, I again yelled with my last shred of dignity spewing onto the track before me, "Cool, well, *I* have a pen and paper." This was partially another lie. I did not have paper, but I did have the palm of my hand, and I stood with my pen, ready to tattoo her information on my body. Probably in awe of my pathetic display (and because who wouldn't have just felt sorry for me at that point?), she turned and walked back toward me. Slowly, she spelled out her email address, watching me, the crazy person before her, press the pen into my hand, willing either ink or blood to begin flowing.

Once I finally let her leave, I assumed I would never see her again.

I waited a day, in an effort not to look desperate, and took around an hour to craft the perfect email to her, which I sent twice for good measure. But the beautiful friendship I had imagined in our earlier hours, unshockingly, never amounted to anything.

I realized during that first year in Portland that making friends post college is a lot like asking someone on a date. You have to put yourself out there. You are nervous, you expect rejection, and you say and do really stupid things. I miss the organic way friendships formed early on in life, like in the sandbox and casually at lunch while drinking a Capri Sun. Now, I have to work for it. I have to struggle. I have to compromise the pace at which I enjoy running, for crying out loud.

Since that fateful day on the track, all of my closest friendships and even my, now, marriage, have developed with housemates and eventually people I met through work. People I have spent years getting close to and who might have just passed me by if we saw each other in line for coffee. A shame, really, so many things work against organic relationships now. I look around at people on their phones while waiting in checkout lines, missing a good five-minute window of conversation that could be had with the person next to them. At coffee shops, I sometimes imagine that everyone on their computer is looking at their online dating profile when they could just look up and see someone, who might even be on that dating site, in person. Maybe these are missed experiences, or maybe those random encounters wouldn't work out anyway. With some, you just have to learn to love us …

HIGH SCHOOL
LOVE

I was nearing the end of my limit in a hot tub at a friend's house when Kyle, a fellow eighth grader, who could have easily passed for a fourth grader until he started talking and the crackling of adulthood tried to push its way into his life via his vocal cords, suggested we play truth or dare. Never one to make a first move of any kind, I was prepared to sit in that tub and wither into the most dehydrated grape before I would get out earlier than the cooler-than-me kids did. An obvious option would have been to simply pull myself onto the side of the tub and relieve my heart from deciding whether thirteen was too young to give up. But, being an eighth-grade girl, I preferred death by hot water to a visible and nearly naked body. And rightfully so—I was not one of those teenage girls who ate the rumored hormonal chicken and developed early. In fact, my gender was only known because I was wearing a two-piece bathing suit rather than swim trunks. I had short hair and a muscular physique, particularly around my chest, which was shaped in a beautiful pectoral formation rather than revealing any signs of breast buds like my female classmates. So there I sat, dying of heat in a disgusting albeit chlorinated tub with about eight other ripe thirteen-year-olds, wondering how long truth or dare would last.

Eighth grade was an interesting time for me. I was not quite pubescent in that I had no boobs nor my period yet, but this did not halt the more visibly unattractive qualities a child going through puberty could have the misfortune of experiencing. A dusting of acne covered my forehead. Just my forehead. I never got the large boil-looking acne, rather tiny red bumps determined to ruin my face pushed their way through my skin for the better half of junior and high school despite my efforts to clear them with every chemical invented. Then there was my body. I had been a gymnast most of my childhood. Though I'd retired years before, my stature was permanently stunted, and the muscles remained. Boobs were trying to make an appearance, but my pecs were, by far, winning the war. Body odor and weird hair in weirder places was appearing in the same way the earliest spring flowers do—by surprise, even though winter suggested they might stay dormant forever, but then one day, there they were, visible and smelling.

I was under no guise that this was what I looked like. I didn't think I was some beautiful flower. I knew in my heart I was the epitome of an awkward teen, and I acted as such, recluse and constantly surprised when someone talked to me at school. So I assumed when truth or dare started in the hot tub and I was one of the first recipients of a challenge, it was some cruel teenage joke.

"Jason, I dare you to kiss Melissa," Kyle said. His words sounded like his mouth was full of marbles, muffled through the extra saliva that his braces seemed to always collect.

Caught off guard, I looked at Jason. I wouldn't have been surprised if they told me to kiss Stuart, a kid on an aesthetically equal playing field. Then it would make sense. We could make our way in the steaming tub toward one another and awkwardly try to navigate my, and what would surely be his, first kiss in front of eight other schoolmates. It would be the talk of the moment for years to come and inevitably land me in therapy twenty years down the road. But no. *Jason* was dared to kiss *me*. Jason was tall for eighth grade and more muscular than me, which seemed important. He had deep brown skin, a face free of zits, and a lot of friends. These things individually equaled award-winning adolescent shit, but combined, he was akin to a purebred *Best in Show* candidate. The only bright side I could see was that if the dare was what was sending nervous sweat out of my pores, the kind that smelled like a dumpster outside of a pho restaurant, surely the other dudes in the tub were covering me as the primary suspect.

Jason looked at me, and I realized I was about to have my first kiss. He had been sitting on the side of the tub like a sane human. I was located on the other side with a jet blowing water straight up the back of my suit, so when I moved forward, the air released from under me, sending large bubbles to the top of the tub. Yes, like a fart would. Luckily, I was entering a state of blackout due to nerves. Jason's six-pack abs flexed as he pushed off the side of the hot tub with his hands behind him and lowered himself into the water to make his way toward me. He took one breaststroke, and we were upon each other. His moisturized lips came toward my severely dehydrated ones. I stood in a half squat in the middle of the hot tub to stay submerged in the water from the neck down. I kept my eyes open just in case this was some big practical joke and I needed to be aware of something flying at my face. He leaned down and toward me, and we had a short two-second kiss as our hands stayed respectfully under water and to ourselves. There was nothing remarkable about the kiss other than it happened. It was exactly like when you practice by putting together your middle and index fingers to simulate kissing lips, only it was wetter and chlorinated. When it ended, everyone clapped. I took a few steps back and let the jet resume cleansing my butt.

The best part of middle school is that if I looked back now at a yearbook, I would see that no one was any better off than me. But as a thirteen-year-old, I only saw my own metamorphosis. I assume an adult onlooker would shield their eyes at the sight of any one of us. The pretty girls weren't even pretty; they just had boobs first. And the cool guys played sports—big whoop. We all had acne and armpits that smelled like they were rotting. End of discussion. So it was to my surprise when my friend Ann told me Jason had set the whole dare situation up. I was shocked. *A popular boy liked me?*

It started in the way eighth-grade love usually does—going to the movies in a large group and sitting next to each other, maybe. It turned into him calling me on the landline a couple evenings a week after school. Any time I heard the phone ring, I would grab it and pull the coiled cord until the wire was taut and I was as far from a family member as possible, crouched on the floor in another room, phone pulled so far it threatened ripping the drywall right from the house.

One night, as we were talking on the phone about how Mr. Jacobson's zipper was down in math class, he asked, "Do you believe in evolution or creationism?"

I'd spent one year in Jewish Sunday school before dropping out. I had zero knowledge or context to answer this question in a way that reflected anything I actually believed. But even if I did, I'm not sure it would have mattered. The thing I remember running through my mind when he asked me this was, *I wonder what he believes in? How can I answer this in a way he will like?* And here's the other rub: I had never once thought about if *I* liked *him*. He liked me, and my concern was only keeping it that way.

"I guess evolution," I said as it was the only of the two I had even heard of at that point. I don't recall his response to that. I only remember sitting in my living room in the dark as I hoped to God I'd picked the right answer to his religious wonderings.

"So would you ever convert?" he asked in that same conversation.

"Convert religions?" I asked, now genuinely confused.

"Yeah. I mean, we can date, but we could never get married or have kids," said the fourteen-year-old boy.

"Why?"

"Well, aren't you concerned you're going to hell because you're Jewish?" His tone was not malicious or even implying I was wrong in my beliefs, just that I would be going to hell, in his mind, because my beliefs did not align with his, or so I understood it. He sounded matter-of-factly concerned for my afterlife.

When I was a kid, my neighbors were deeply Christian. Meaning, to me at the time, they went to church every Sunday. I was best friends with them, and during the summers, I couldn't understand why they got to go to camp at the church and I was left home with only my barbies to keep me company. So one summer, after what I am sure amounted to many tantrums, my mom said I could go to bible camp with them. There's not much I remember being that different than any other camp I had been to. We played archery outside, ate hot dogs and those popsicle tubes with neon colors too impossibly bright to be safely edible. But one day of camp sticks out in my head. We were inside, all sitting in folding chairs, watching the pastor give a speech at the front. Must've been the religious portion of the day because when I tuned in, it was because he was asking who had been "saved." We were instructed to raise our hands if we hadn't been. With my hand in the air, I wondered if it counted when I was saved from being bitten by a dog at around age six. Not remembering what happened in the interim, I was soon being led to the front with a few others who apparently had the misfortune of not being safe in life either. Before I knew it, I was repeating after him. *Something, something, something ...* "Yes, I let Jesus into my life ..." And with that, I guessed I was safe. Later at camp, I repeated the ceremony, assuming if I did it twice for good measure, I would be even safer.

The year Jason told me I was going to hell, we had learned "if-then" statements in math. One kid, when asked for an example, said, "If you fart, then it will smell." To him, in his life experience, this was clearly true. But not everyone's farts smell, and so there arose some debate to the validity of his statement. Jason had learned in church that *if* you weren't Christian, *then* you were going to hell. This wasn't my learned experience, but he believed it so deeply that he felt it appropriate to point out to me, his eighth-grade girlfriend, that we wouldn't be procreating on account of my being Jewish and I was going to hell, lest I convert.

I'd like to tell you that this was the moment I realized I could have my own mind. That I moved forward from that phone call asking myself if I liked the people I dated.

Instead, I spent my teenage years framing relationships in the same way I did with Jason—not ever thinking about what I wanted. I would sit in a tub of boiling water and nearly pass out before I risked letting boys see the imperfections I saw in my morphing adolescent body. I would date someone solely because he liked me and never thought to wonder if I liked him back. And in the end, it would never be enough; I would never be enough for them. If only then I knew that one day I would grow up and realize that none of that mattered. As cheesy and cliché as it sounds, and with no way better to say it, one day, I would realize the only thing that matters is *if* I am enough for myself, *then* I have everything I need. I wouldn't develop that perspective for some time, but eventually, I would get there and, apparently, even if I slipped up and forgot once in a while, it probably wouldn't matter because, hell, I was doubly safe.

GAY DATING

t was the final night around the campfire after a week-long adventure down the Deschutes River where twenty students and I had just been trained to be river guides. Appreciating the flames warming my leathered face, I stared at each new friend coming in and out of view as the fire danced in the middle of us. I've never preferred the type of dirty felt after a long day of work in the city, tired from motionlessness and needing to shower off the smell of office donuts and regret. Being outside all day, bones and muscles fatigued from movement, face tight after being in and out of the sun and water for hours on end was way more appealing to me.

The short story of how I ended up at raft guide training was a result of an even shorter conversation I'd had with Emily, my friend and housemate at the time, who had been working for the rafting company going on twenty years.

Emily and I were having breakfast together one morning, the winter before guide training. As normally as one might have asked of my day's plans, she swallowed a bite of oatmeal, and without looking up, said, "Melissa, you're going to go through guide training in April."

Confused, I replied, "What?"

"Yeah, you heard me," she said as she got up from the table to put her dish in the sink. She rinsed it off, put it in the drying rack then turned back toward me. "Got better things going on?"

I sat silent at the table, watching her put her bike helmet on and secure her bag around her waist.

She reached for the back door and looked over at me. "Gotta go!" And she was gone to work for the day.

Suddenly by myself, I snickered at the thought, crossing my arms and sulking down in my chair as I huffed air out of my nose. I quickly realized not only did I not have "better things" going on, I had *nothing* going on.

A few months later, I found myself a river guide, sitting at a fire with twenty new friends. It's really no more interesting than that.

After probably thirty minutes staring at the flames, I was jolted up by a cold beer dropped onto my lap. "Drink up!" someone said as they passed by me en route to making sure everyone had a full can. Soon, the sounds of popping flames were intertwined with the almost as frequent sounds of beer cans being flattened in the dirt under the weight of Chaco sandals.

"Melissa! Over here!" Val, another housemate of mine who had also come on the training, called to me. I leaned back in my camp chair and noticed a small group had formed, set a ways away from the fire with a few guys, Val, and Lindsey.

Lindsey. If I had to describe her appearance in a word, it would, without hesitation, be *hot*. Not a very feminist way of me to describe another woman, but sometimes, it just is what it is. And Lindsey was hot. She just was. Boys thought it, girls thought it, probably woodland creatures thought it, too. In every rom-com, there is the girl next door—let's call her Mary—who ultimately wins the guy. Then there is the girl who the guy cheats on Mary with—let's call her Tanya—who is a little more worldly, mysterious, has a "story," and is so painfully hot that you can't quite look directly at her. Lindsey was Tanya. She was also a badass. During the week of training, it was quickly known by everyone that she would become a full-time guide. In guide training, this was like the equivalent of the person you knew in high school who would probably go to an Ivy League. She was the first girl I met who smashed the notion of what it meant to be a "pretty girl." Where I came from, in the Midwest, pretty girls did not tie knots or guide rafts in whitewater. They certainly didn't pee into the river underneath their sarongs without a second thought, and under no circumstances would they poop on top of everyone else's poop in a large ammo can with a rationed square of toilet paper to clean up with, as we did during training.

It was a strange setup, this private group set back behind some trees all formed in a small circle. They all opened the circle enough to let me in. My confusion over what was going on was soon cleared up. "Val and Lindsey were just going to make out!" Steven, another drunk student within this secret circle, slurred.

Just like that, I looked over, and Lindsey started kissing Val, and everyone cheered and held up their near-empty beer cans while it happened. *Holy shit.* I stood there confused but following suit with my beer in the air.

Once they parted, "Now kiss Melissa!" Steven and Lindsey yelled to Val.

"No way!" Val and I both said in unison. "Dude, we're roommates," Val explained.

"Fine, then Melissa kiss Lindsey!" Steven yelled, nearly toppling over.

Instantly, my stomach felt like it was going to fall out of my butt. I was standing in this weird circle wearing dirty track pants, the same shirt I'd been wearing for a week, and a grimy bandana that was holding my hair back, though it could have held itself back. I registered blurry beer cans in the air as I looked over at Lindsey. I'd kissed plenty of boys before, but none had ever made me feel simultaneously like Christmas morning and puking. Kissing boys was robotic. It was what I was supposed to do. Boys kissed girls. Just like that. That was what I knew.

In the seconds between suggestion and reality, I found time to wonder a surprising number of things. *Should I run away?* There was a whole forest behind us, and I could make myself scarce in about two minutes. Everyone would be too drunk to chase me, and I could live out the rest of my days in the woods. *Fuck, did I even brush my teeth this morning?* Likely not. *Should I just faint?* Right there, just drop to the ground, thus avoiding the whole thing. But I didn't move. With each thought I had about avoiding it, I solidly wanted it even more.

Suddenly, I felt her lips hit mine. That moment was like those initial half lucid minutes during an afternoon nap when your normal thoughts morph into impossible realities, signaling you're sort of asleep and definitely not fully awake. After the initial contact, the kiss became instinctual. Specifics regarding the group's visual wishes—tongue, no tongue, etc.—had not been discussed. We met somewhere closer to the end of the full-on making out spectrum than kissing your mom goodbye on the first day of school's end. Once contact was made, our mouths parted just a little, and we shared the beginnings of first-date "gentle" kissing. Then I remember very vividly biting her bottom lip lightly, something I had never done before, tugging on it slightly with my teeth before placing one hand on her back, pulling our bodies closer as we kissed for a few seconds longer. Apparently, dirty track pants were my superhero cape. It lasted for roughly a year—or five seconds—I can't remember. Soon our lips came apart, but I wasn't finished. Forgetting our audience, I leaned back in, already craving this thing that brought me more into the present than I had ever felt. Then it ended. I just stood there frozen, again, but no longer wanting to vomit.

"You're a good kisser," she said, her inflection revealing a hint of surprise.

As soon as it started, our little circle broke up, and everyone went back to warm by the fire. I made my way over and sat back in my chair, drunk and confused but ultimately setting that experience aside for years and suppressing the want to answer the question in my mind: *Why did I like that?*

Our bodies are designed to protect us from harm, internal and external. We have physiological responses to danger, mechanisms in our brain and chemicals released that help us not feel pain. My mind let the rest of me in on the news that I was gay when I was twenty-seven—a good four years after that kiss. It was seemingly out of nowhere, as if I were reading a book peacefully in a quiet corner with a mug of Celestial Seasons, and suddenly, a train rolls by, sounding its horn, jarring me from the imaginary world of what I was reading. Just like that, I was hit on the back of the head, jolted from my safe alternative reality with the realization—*Holy shit, I'm gay!*

There were certainly signs, like experiencing a meditative state while kissing a girl and friends who said to me a million times, "Are you sure you aren't gay?" But as my greatest protector, my brain wouldn't hear it until I was ready.

I quickly went onto OkCupid. I'd wasted enough time. I secured my first ever gay date with another woman named Jane. We talked back and forth for a week or so via instant messages before deciding to meet in person. She learned in those initial conversations that I had never dated a woman before and, to my surprise, she still wanted to meet me.

There was nothing special to me about Jane. Her name was as plain as she was. That was why I wanted to meet her. If I was going to take this new part of myself into a public space, outside of where it was protected in my brain and within my computer, I needed her to be neutral. I could not yet compound it with real feelings. I wasn't quite ready to bring this part of me that still felt black and white into full color. We met one afternoon at a coffee shop. I couldn't tell you what she was wearing, probably a gray t-shirt, bootcut jeans, and Dansko clogs. She had brown hair, brown eyes, and pale skin. She wasn't ugly and she wasn't pretty.

I was early, as I generally am, so I ordered a decaf coffee and found a seat in the corner of the cafe. I wanted to be out of sight, realizing this would be the first time I would publicly be with another woman who didn't fit neatly into the friendship box. Looking down at my coffee thinking about what I would say to start the date off, I heard a bell at the door jingle and looked up to see her walk in. She took two steps toward me, and I immediately knew, as I had anticipated and even wanted, that this would be our last time talking. She came over to the table, and as though I were an old friend who she met twice monthly to catch up with for coffee, she threw her stuff down on the chair without a hello and said, "I'm just going to get a drink real quick."

Once seated, Jane got herself situated. She had an odd confidence about her, and I was immediately jealous of it. She brought her mug to her mouth and looked at me while she sipped her coffee. Her eyes seemed to say that she felt sorry for me. That she had all the answers and knew I had none.

"Well, have you kissed a girl?" she demanded right away.

Confused but somehow feeling like I had to answer, I said, "Yes, once."

"But you haven't dated a girl at all, right?"

Looking down at my hands in my lap, I quickly told myself the narrative I wanted to hear so I could dismiss this interaction the moment I left. I told myself I was an anomaly to her. That she only agreed to meet with me because she wanted to see for herself, in the flesh, a twenty-seven-year-old who had no idea she was gay. I put my own embarrassment of myself off on her. "Like I told you, I've never had a girlfriend."

Staring me straight in the eye, she said, "How do you know you're gay then?"

I responded only by squinting my eyes in disbelief at her.

She pressed on proudly. "So you haven't even gone on a date with a woman? Like not at all? I'm your first?" she *said* more than she asked.

"You're my first."

She paused, huffed some breath out, looked at me hard, and said, as if she were letting me in on the greatest kept secret of all time, "Well, let me tell you, women are crazy ..."

I left utterly defeated. I went home to my best friend and roommate at the time, Naime, and cried on her floor. Naime and I had just moved into a basement apartment in Portland, Oregon. She had recently moved back to the city after ending a five-year relationship. It is easy to be depressed during the rainy season in Portland, but add living in a basement to breakups and newly discovered homosexuality, and tears and darkness will fill every corner.

Naime lay in bed looking down at me. "Maybe it's too soon for you to try dating. Maybe you should just get used to the idea first," she said supportively.

"I am not just going to lay in this cold basement alone *thinking* about being gay."

I picked myself up and got into bed, opening my computer once again.

OkCupid wasn't necessarily a means for me to meet a partner at that time. But it was a space where I could be gay among other gays for the first time in my life, even if just in a virtual setting. I could be witty, I could initiate conversation, I could be all the things I wanted to be in real life, but in my pajamas, with food on my face, and without shame.

Next, I got a date with a bisexual named Mary. A really pretty bisexual. She could pick from the whole world, and she picked me.

Hours before my date with Mary, I sat alone in the basement reeling; what if she asked me about my past? What if she sucked? What if she was awesome? Her profile evoked more of an actual interest for me than Jane's had. Shaking my thoughts, I got out the vodka, an alcohol I loved in a completely healthy and in-control sort of way. I generally only drank in excess once a year, at Thanksgiving, the time of year when I was around my family who, because of this, assumed I had a drinking problem. It was talked about and expressed in concerned comments to me whenever I went home for the holidays. Rightfully so, as one year at Thanksgiving, out of nowhere, I called my Aunt Jean a slut in front of the whole table after a few too many. As a joke, my brother-in-law gave me a handle of Vodka for my birthday the next year, and my mom got mad, calling him an enabler, and tried to force an intervention.

This time, even though a holiday wasn't demanding it, I needed a drink. I poured a glass—a pint glass—of vodka on ice. Naime wasn't home. I needed her level head to tell me to put down the sixteen ounces of straight alcohol. I kept drinking. By the time I needed to leave, I was unable to drive. So I biked over to the bar, thinking that would be safer.

I sat and waited, going between the bathroom and the lounge area at least five times to see if the red, inebriated look had drained from my face. As I emerged from the bathroom for a fifth time, she was walking in the door—twenty-five minutes late. She extended her hand. "Are you Melissa?"

"Yes, you must be Mary. Nice to meet you." I went in for a hug, not knowing what else to do. To my benefit, the lights were dim, so hopefully she could see neither my red face nor blotchy eye makeup, but she probably smelled the alcohol.

Mary was beautiful. She had blondish red hair, freckles all over her face, and blue eyes. She wore tight jeans and wedge sandals with a bohemian top. She looked nothing like Lindsey from guide training, but the attraction was the same.

After around two hours of small talk, I grabbed the check. I didn't want to be the one to pay for these drinks in an "I'm the man" sort of way. I anticipated that splitting it would be awkward; I knew—I *knew*—if she paid, which it didn't seem like she was going to do, I would surely say something I'd regret. I get uncomfortable when people do things for me and would probably say something like "Oh, now I gotta get you back" or "Thank you," followed by either a thumbs up or two finger pistols shooting fake bullets at her bewildered face then holstering my hands in my pockets. I couldn't bear it. Not that day. So I paid, and if she took it to be too forward, so be it, but I couldn't have the alternative. She simply said, "Thank you."

We walked out together, and once at the door, I turned to her. "This was so fun," I said.

"Yes, thank you again for the beers." This time, she leaned in for a hug, and I awkwardly followed suit.

We walked toward our bikes, obviously parked next to each other. *Eye roll—FML*. Serendipitously, I thought now, outside, away from the bustle of the restaurant, we might share a kiss. I quickly ensured that would never happen by narrating my next actions: "Just gotta unlock this," I said while fumbling with my keys. Then, "Safety first" as I placed my bright orange helmet on, simultaneously hating myself. Then, as though I hadn't said quite enough, "I like your bike," and I sped away as if at the starting line of the Tour De France, hoping a car would hit me on my way home.

I got home, and Naime was there waiting for details. I really liked Mary. I had no idea how she felt. I replayed the scenes in my head—a few awkward things and not the best parting, and, yes, I was drunk and a bit sweaty at the start, but maybe she didn't catch on to any of that. It could've gone well in her eyes, too. I brought up her profile on Facebook to show Naime and pretended like I didn't care whether I heard from her again. "Yeah, she's cute, but I could go either way," I lied.

I texted her the next day. She never responded.

My third date was with the wittiest woman I have ever talked with. She was a tiny, (like five feet tall), African American woman with soft, kind features that made me want to spill my whole life story to her in place of simply "Hello." She had her hair pulled back and wore jeans and an old t-shirt and sneakers. We met for ice cream one hot summer evening. We each got a cone and walked through a nearby neighborhood, laughing as we worked to lick the cones faster than the summer heat could melt them.

"So, what's your story?" I asked.

She started to tell me about her conservative family. "My brother is the only one who doesn't care I'm gay ... I'm from Texas," she told me as we walked. I pictured myself going home with her to Texas. A gay Jewish girl, when all they wanted for their daughter was for her to marry a nice man who would support her and their offspring—a boy and a girl.

"I don't know if my family cares," I admitted comfortably to her.

"You can come out to them, but it won't make it easier. You just have to keep coming out to everyone you meet after that ..."

I learned she was right. Being gay isn't like being a minority because of your race. You typically don't see the gayness. There are stereotypes you can make a good guess on, but you wouldn't see me walking down the street and immediately know I'm gay. So I look for a hint of acceptance in everyone I meet, carefully discerning if it's safe to let them know that part of me. Straight until told otherwise.

Each woman I went on a date with was the opposite of the one previous. I was proving to myself, in an unintended experiment in gay-dating, that there is no "type" of person that is gay. It could be anyone. Being gay isn't abnormal.

I'm not weird, I tell myself daily.

People often ask, "How did you just jump right into dating?" or "Aren't you scared of rejection?" or say, "I could never go through all those bad dates …" If I were simply online looking for a mate, I might have thought more about those things. I spent countless hours, countless nights, in my bed in that basement scrolling through a community of women who had, more or less, at some point, experienced what I was trying to make sense of. With each one, I found a little more clarity in my own situation. I wasn't looking for the perfect partner; I was searching for stories like mine. I didn't need someone to love; I needed an example in someone that could let me know it was okay to love this new part of myself. I wanted that meditative state somewhere between lucid and dreaming to come back, not in the ease of one kiss, but in how I lived my new life.

WINNING
THE GOLD

When I was a kid, I wanted one thing: to be an Olympic champion. I would watch the athletes take the field for the opening ceremonies and see them through their Olympic journeys, either fulfilling or crushing their respective dreams. I sat in amazement, taking on their pain and joy as if it were my own. We, I in front of my TV and the athletes on the field, would all come together at the end, no matter the outcome, for the closing ceremonies. And this unification is why the Olympic games are so great. They are what brings our otherwise angry world together to watch and celebrate something common.

As it happened, I found myself at twenty-six, not an Olympian, but working nights as a waitress at a jazz club.

After an evening shift at the club, as the staff all counted our tips, Ken, the manager, called a meeting to tell us all, "Sorry guys, the restaurant is closing down in a month."

The owner of the club, Jim, was an older man. Jazz was all he ever knew in life, and it seemed he opened the club just so he would have a place to sit and eat a prime rib dinner while watching his favorite musicians. At least that was all I ever observed him doing while I wasn't waiting on him at a table in my section for the tip he never left.

Truth be told, I was tired of the service industry. It was not the path to stardom I had envisioned for myself when dreams were had at eight years old. By twenty-six, I had worked sporadically in restaurants for roughly ten years, which led me to a conclusion on the subject of human behavior: People generally suck.

I live under the assumption that if people suck, they should be told immediately and in the most blatant form possible. I also live under the practice of never saying anything, lest it come in a note, email, sarcastic comment, or some other passive-aggressive form. Somewhere in the middle of these two extremes is where my ideal world resides. But in customer service, everything is answered with a smile, and we are happy to perform anything asked of us. Pick the julienned tomatoes out of your pasta? *Of course!* Listen to you tell me why I am horrible at my job and as a person? *Bring it on. I love feedback!* And we take it. Every shift, we take it because if we don't, we don't get paid. But what would change if you knew you couldn't be fired, if you knew you could probably get away with anything … What would you do? What would you *say*? In modern times, electronic screens serve as walls between us and the real world of conversation—facial expression, debate, and any other forms of rebuttal that make our skin collectively crawl just imagining them. The story will no longer go, "When I was your age, I had to *walk* to school in the snow, fifteen feet of it!" It will soon become something more along the lines of, "When I was your age, I had to *talk* to people just to *communicate*!"

Friday night, my second to last shift, live music was playing, the fryers were frying, and the servers were running. As I took in the scene from the back of the restaurant, in walked a woman whose makeup you could scratch off with your fingernail, leaving a canyon down her face. I approached her thinking about this. She made direct eye contact with me while shouting, "Hi five!"

Confused, thinking she actually wanted a high five and having done nothing impressive so far to warrant it, I just sort of stared at her. She then slowed her words so my, what she probably assumed was a very small, server brain could understand her.

"Table ..." two-second pause, "for ..." two-second pause, "five."

Realizing she wanted a table for five people, I grabbed some menus and showed her to her seat. What proceeded was, more or less, the standard. She and her friends wanted wine but weren't sure which kind. So, being a professional, I offered them samples. Each time I arrived with a new sample, I watched as they swirled the glass, tipped the contents down their throats, then, "Now, a taste of the Malbec" (repeat procedure) and "How about the Syrah?" working their way down the wine list until completing what amounted to a full glass in tastes and about a mile of walking back and forth for me. Then, ultimately, in the end, "You know what, I'll just have a gin and tonic." They all nodded at each other in agreement.

While she and her friends weren't especially polite, they were drinking a lot. At this club, an automatic cover charge was added to everyone's bill while live music was playing. I added this and watched their bill, and, subsequently, my tip and mood increase with each "gin, two ice cubes and half a lime (no please or thank you)" they downed. All was fairly normal for the three hours they were there enjoying the music. Toward the end of the night, I looked over at their table, and the woman in charge gave me the universal outstretched palm with the finger scribing on it—*I want my check.* Too far away to say anything, I gave them the universal hand indication that I would be right there—one finger up but never the one we wanted.

I turned my back to print their check just as I heard the woman yell over the music. "Well, I guess I just won't pay then!"

Delivering the check to their table with a hastened kick in my step, a "Thank you!" and a fake smile, I mused all the passive aggressive notes I wanted to leave for her. Instead, I went about delivering a few of their plates to the dish room, not wanting to hover as they sorted their payment. I returned to find a pile of cash and a gift certificate on the table.

Ken walked over and looked down at the pile. "Did they tip you?" he asked curiously, invested in this table, as I'd been complaining to him about them for the last three hours.

Before this, not thinking that they might not, I said, "I don't know" as Ken grabbed the pile and counted it for me.

He glanced back at the total on the check. "It's not enough to cover the bill." Ken said this with a hint of excited undertones, possibly already musing what I might do.

He was fully aware of my mood that night. I counted it and came to the same conclusion. Then I thought, *This is what we've always wanted*. It didn't matter what I might say; the place was closing down in two days. I started running out the door to catch them, but as I made it on the sidewalk, I realized I should double check because how embarrassing would it be to get to them having just done the math wrong.

I called over to Ken, and we both did the math again.

Looking fiercely into Ken's eyes, I declared, "I'm doing it." And we both knew I had never meant anything more in my life.

As if I were some lead in a movie and he was my captain sending me off to war, he ordered, "Do what you have to do."

I took off, immediately spotting them a couple blocks away. I started sprinting. This is what I had been training for. This was for everyone who had ever stiffed me or a co-worker. This was for everyone who worked silently, letting themselves get talked to like shit. This was for the servers of the world! With each person, I decided this "was for" my speed increased. So much so that soon, I saw their backs right in front of me, and as I skidded to a stop, I realized I had no idea what I was going to actually say. Then something inside me took over. "Hey!" I yelled, shocking even myself. They turned, all five of them, not at all expecting me to be there in my dirty apron, hair askew from the sprint and adrenaline-crazed expression taking over every part of my face.

Shaking. "You didn't pay your whole bill," I yelled a little too loudly, still amped. In my head, everyone in the street had stopped and was now staring at us.

The ringleader stepped forward. "Yes, we did." This was not her first time.

I explained that they, in fact, did not, and they told me they refused to pay the cover charge for the music that was added to all the patrons' bills.

"You sat and listened to the band for three hours, and you think you don't have to pay the cover?" My voice nervously cracked like a pubescent boy.

"Yeah, well, we weren't told about the cover." She said this like it was something she had said a hundred times before. I wanted her confidence.

Deep breath. "It is outside on the sign. It is on another sign at eye level on the door you walked through, and it is on all the tables. You knew. So you are just going to steal from the band then?" I thought perhaps if I added another moral element to the equation they would concede.

"We're not paying it." She said this, proving my "people generally suck" theory as she took a step forward and stared straight into my soul.

"Well," I started. Then a pause as I tried to gather my thoughts and come up with some brilliant line that would haunt their dreams forever. "Well, you guys are all *assholes*." I said "assholes" to a customer's face with the power of one hundred "assholes" behind it.

Do I wish I had come up with something better, more clever? Obviously. But they *were* assholes. I went against ten years of customer service experience. I took that ten years and said "assholes" to them with enough intention that I felt like I'd called everyone who had ever been an asshole to me an asshole.

Not waiting for any of them to reply, I turned back toward the restaurant and broke into a light jog. I couldn't have walked if I wanted to. It felt like what I had always imagined the aftermath of setting a new Olympic record might feel like. Unlike that, there wasn't anyone to visibly cheer me on, but I knew I had thousands behind me on my team. Probably no one in the restaurant but Ken even knew I was gone, but I didn't care. I opened the door and walked back out on the floor like I had dreamed when I was eight that I might enter the stadium of the Olympic ceremonies. That night, I won my gold.

SLINGSHOTS

When I was ten, the movie *It Takes Two,* starring Mary Kate and Ashley Olsen, came out. I really identified, or wanted to identify, with Mary Kate, who played Amanda. Amanda was then described as a tomboy, but now, in a more politically correct world, I would call her a dirty girl. Meh, that sounds weird, too. She was a girl who wasn't afraid of getting rough and tumble and generally liked stereotypical boy things. I didn't know much at that age, but after seeing that movie, there were two things I knew for sure: 1) I needed a slingshot. 2) I would exclusively wear overalls for the rest of my good years.

A few weeks after, I'd amassed roughly eighty-four viewings of *It Takes Two,* and my grade school class had just finished reading *The Adventures of Huckleberry Finn.* Since we were in Missouri, we took a field trip to Hannibal, the home of Huck himself, where I knew there would be a gift shop rife with what dreams were made of—slingshots.

We were given one instruction during our free time in Hannibal: Don't buy toy weapons. So I bought a slingshot. It slung perfectly in the hammer loop of my overalls upon purchase—in plain sight. The fact that I was found out was the main infraction I saw about the whole operation. My new slingshot was confiscated and taken back to school where my parents were involved in a way I'm not privy to but somehow resulted in my being able to keep the slingshot so long as it was never at school. I spent my afternoons and weekends perched in a tree in our front lawn—overalls on, weapon holstered, and rocks in all my pockets.

When I look back at photos during this time, I notice the shirts under my overalls were quite girly, either in color (pink) or detail (fringe around the neck and sleeves). There was always something about my outfit that signified to a passerby, *That's a girl*. I can almost see my mom, the type of woman who would emerge each day from the house only after an hour spent peering into a small vanity mirror, working at her face like Picasso, scanning me while looking for a way to bring out some femininity in my dress. The overalls weren't cutting it, duh! My body didn't do it; I was oddly muscular as a child. And my hair? Think not Winnie but Kevin Arnold of *The Wonder Years*. I didn't want to be a boy when I was a kid; I just observed that boys were allowed more fun. *It Takes Two* seemed to portray how I saw it quite nicely: Amanda being labeled a tom*boy* meant she got to play outside and get dirty and crush sloppy joes for dinner. Alyssa had to play the piano, wear dresses, and eat snails. Oh, sorry—escargot.

I stayed this way for awhile. Actually, it is fair to say I am this way still. I literally just flicked a dead fly off my dirty pant leg as I typed this tale, and I'm thirty-three. But at some point, it becomes not as *okay* to wear dirty overalls and holster a slingshot on your person at all times. Somewhere along the way, I was supposed to want to trade in my weapon, my protection, for things that felt more fragile to me, things that, to me, signified womanhood like bras and tampons. My other friends at the time could be described as very girly, with their long, silky hair and monogrammed overnight bags.

On another school field trip that same year, we went to a play. I have zero recollection which play; in fact, I'm fairly sure I only watched the back of the seat in front of me after what proceeded. My friends wore skirts and dresses with ponytails, and I wore a black cable knit sweater that had red flowers stitched down the front, pleated khaki pants, and my Kevin Arnold haircut. In front of us sat a group of boys from another school dressed quite similarly to me, save for the floral prints. One of them turned to face our row and looked me up and down.

"Why don't you dress like your friends?" he asked.

I stayed mute.

"Why don't you have long hair like your friends?" another turned and questioned.

Still mute.

The boys laughed amongst themselves.

My friends told them to stop in words I can't recall, and one of them told a teacher, who pulled me aside later that day to embarrass me further by asking if I was okay. Of course, I was *okay*. But I was also confused. This is now where I can pinpoint my first confrontation with the stifling stereotypes and gendered structures of our culture, though I didn't understand it at the time: I was not conforming correctly to being a girl. I was not fitting into the image of what a girl should look like to them. That made the boys uncomfortable.

In my youth, *normal* was boys getting dirty and girls playing with dolls. *Normal* was teenage girls wearing makeup and having crushes on boys while teenage boys pretended to be big and strong and hide all their feelings. *Normal* was a white picket fence. *Normal* was women and men getting married. *Normal* meant everybody stayed comfortable and no one was challenged. Like believing in Santa, we slowly lose our childhood innocence over time. We believe in Santa—insist on him and his magic—until our belief is shaken by seemingly innocuous events that, over time, erode it away. One friend tells us he saw his dad put presents under the tree. *No way*, a kid thinks. Another friend saw their mom buying the doll they swore they'd only told Santa about. *It can't be.* The next year, little Tommy saw the carrots he'd left out for the reindeer in the kitchen trash. *Something isn't right.*

With each new experience in adolescence, our innocence drips away until it's lost. We stay in a land of learned normalcy for a while, but with any luck, somewhere along the line, we might begin to wake up and realize the innocence of childhood might be way better for the world.

I turned thirteen and spent the better part of that year trying to figure out the engineering of a tampon—the worst possible thing I thought could happen to me. Then the second most unspeakable thing happened to my body. My actual worst nightmares were realized: respectively, having boobs, admitting to having boobs, and wearing something that gave away having boobs.

As I grew older, so, too, did my role models. Coming of age, one of my favorite movies was *Now and Then*. I was equally fascinated with adolescence as I was learning how to keep myself out of it. Roberta, one of the main characters in *Now and Then*, would tape her boobs every morning before leaving the house. I vowed to do the same should I ever grow some of my own.

Then it happened.

I was climbing into the car after school, and my mom turned to me. "Melissa, we are going bra shopping this weekend," she all but sang with glee.

I wanted to tell Mom that all we actually needed to do was visit the local hardware store for some heavy-duty duct tape (okay, Scotch tape would suffice), but my mom, a classy lady, would never have gone for it. Shame.

To give my mom credit, it was probably the appropriate time for me to get ahold of a bra anyway. I'd just started the seventh grade, the first year we all changed for gym class in front of one another. As the only girl in eyeshot without an appropriate holster for my non-existent chest, I'd been sparing myself the indignity of my peers' stares and seeking refuge in one of the bathroom stalls to change in every afternoon.

Once my fate as a new bra owner was inevitable, I came up with my terms of purchase. "Fine, but we don't need help. I don't need to be measured, promise?" I pleaded, looking her dead in the eye.

"I promise," she said almost convincingly.

We walked into the shop and were immediately greeted by exactly who you are probably picturing in your head right now. "How can I help you?" a middle-aged woman, likely named Nancy, whose makeup I could chisel away at for hours before unearthing her face, said a little too loudly. She wore thick, floral perfume. Her eyes seemed to twinkle at the prospect of humiliating the next breast-budding girl to walk through the department store doors, and mine watered as her scent invaded my face. Obviously, this is probably only how I am *choosing* to remember her. I'm sure she was lovely.

Without hesitation, "Oh, my daughter here needs to be measured for her first bra!" Linda, the woman I was with, formerly known as *Mom,* said loudly enough so the whole mall now knew what we were up to that Sunday before we hit Auntie Anne's for a pretzel. Linda kept eye contact with Nancy. I died inside.

"Perfect!" Nancy exclaimed.

A tape measure hung lazily around her neck. She had glasses with a delicate gold chain attached so she could remove them and let them sink into her cleavage as she squinted closer to try locating any semblance of a chest beneath my pectoral muscles. She ushered me into a changing room, pushing my shoulders lightly as my head stayed turned to stare at Linda directly in the eyes, letting her know we were over as a partnership.

Once the French dressing room doors shut behind us, Nancy slung the tape measure around my ribs as a formality; she probably thought I was excited to be there. That, like most girls I knew, I had been *waiting* to get to wear a bra, that she was doing me a favor by acting like I needed to be measured. All I wanted was for her to say something along the lines of, "Oh! You don't need a bra, dear! And look how strong you are! You can just continue to wear that undershirt; check back in a few years." Instead, after not much consideration from Nancy, I was relegated to wearing a cotton "training bra" as they called it. But what was I training for? Womanhood? Covering myself?

Perhaps these are normal stories. Girl procures slingshot. Girl gets told she isn't girly enough. Girl learns about period from the pamphlet that comes in the box. Girl needs bra. Girl changes in a bathroom stall so no one knows about it. Growing up, for me, was a lot about hiding. Too much about hiding. I've always thought it was my nature as a shy person to be private, but looking back, it's what I was taught from the minute things started shifting from childhood.

I didn't want the responsibility of "womanhood," so I was cool hiding behind it, ashamed of my new parts.

I'm still learning in my thirties what I wish I was taught at twelve—that what's actually *normal* and not worth hiding is who we become after childhood. That we do a disservice to ourselves by implying anything else. Before the boys at the play had made fun of me, I didn't think anything I was wearing was out of the ordinary. But after that day, I became like those boys for a while, thinking I was different, and different meant weird, and differences were to be hidden. That day, I fell somewhere between the two learned categories of what men and women look like. I wasn't what they understood. I made them uncomfortable. So they took their learned behavior and thrust it into my naive world where I thought I could be whatever I wanted, and in five minutes, they made me doubt it all. Nothing could have protected me from those boys, not even a slingshot.

My story isn't unique. It's as "normal" as girls dressed in pink and boys in blue. It may not be your story, but I'm willing to bet any woman has one with lines that can be drawn next to mine. Probably someone told you what you look like or what you wear isn't right; how you act should be different; you should be more this or that, less of something or another. If I have a kid, that's what they'll learn about first; and should I have a boy (please, God, no), I'll probably buy him tampons for his twelfth birthday, put two lawn chairs out front, sit him down and talk to him a little too loudly about bra shopping and my first period.

HUMAN RAGE

There are two daily instances in which we set aside who we are and assume the worst possible versions of ourselves: on the road and behind a computer screen. Both provide a barrier between us and the person we are engaging with.

If you've ever wasted the better half of an evening scrolling through social media comments on public posts then you understand the depths of human nature when no repercussions for a person's words are at stake. Just yesterday, I read a man's comment to a woman calling her a "cunt-whore" because she supported a liberal presidential candidate. He spelled cunt "cnt," I believe, intentionally because, apparently, you can't just write that whole word out on the Internet. That would be mean. But that is honestly kitten's play compared to the thousands of opinions people blast on everything from moisturizer to actual real-life issues like which organic dog food is best. Much to my chagrin, I often fall down the hole of reading these comments like they're Shakespearean prose—unable to understand them and completely enthralled.

I like to imagine who the people are in real life writing these comments. *What are their lives like?* When I see a particularly nasty one, I like to click on their profile. Generally, his profile pic is some version of him swinging his four-year-old child around in the yard with a golden retriever chasing closely behind. Bubbles float in the air that his wife is blowing into the wind from her seat on a handmade quilt, upon which a beautiful picnic is spread as she watches her perfect family and strokes her pregnant belly.

At night, once everyone is asleep, I imagine he commences his other life as a troll. He slides out from under his 1,000-thread-count sheets but not before kissing Rebecca (as I assume is his wife's name) lightly on the forehead. He slips on his moccasins, ties his silk robe then tip toes into his office in the room next door where the light from his computer screen twinkles in his squinted, ever-angering eyes. It is here that he can let loose, say what he wants, get angry. He doesn't have to be a perfect picture of a fucked up American dream. He can call a woman an "f-ing cnt," spell nothing right, confuse *their* with *they're* and probably get hundreds of likes depending on the platform, sending a dopamine rush to his little brain, validating this version of himself deep within while Rebecca sleeps soundly and unaware in the next room.

Road rage is similar if not slightly more real in that you actually see the person in real life whom you are offending. To me, road rage taps into a more immediate feeling of rage. Online reading others' comments can numb the senses, and after a few hours of scrolling, whatever you have to say probably doesn't seem quite as bad as the dude five lines up who called someone a "dick-loving monster whore." So people say what they have to say then shut their computers, push the golden retriever off the bed, and count monsters to put themselves to sleep.

But what is it about a steel car frame that makes people feel invisible? I was driving in a large thunderstorm one night, minding my own business, listening to Katy Perry just slightly too loud but totally paying attention to the road in front of me. I was in the process of checking my surroundings, preparing to merge onto the highway. A car already on the highway was going about my same speed in the lane next to me, preventing a smooth merge. I started to slow down to tuck in behind him. I looked up, and his middle finger was pressed up as closely to the passenger window as he could get it and still drive. Confused, I squinted at him, tried to slow down, and pull behind him. He wouldn't let me over and started signaling by grabbing an invisible handle and making a circular motion, telling me to roll down my window in my apparently early 1980s vehicle. He angrily slowed down enough so I could go in front of him, then he came as close to the back bumper as he could. He angrily swerved to my side and mouthed, "Pull over" and shot up his middle finger again. At this point, I was genuinely confused about what I'd done wrong. I sped up, got off at the next exit and went about my night. But WTF? Why do people get so angry at small infractions in a vehicle? Is it that their car is really important to them? I don't think so. Is it that they had a bad day at work? Maybe.

But here's where my fascination begins—I have never had a stranger give me the finger because I accidentally bumped into them on the sidewalk. In that case, generally, both people are quick to say, "Oh, sorry!" I have never had someone give me the finger because I went into the express lane at the grocery store with thirteen items—an infraction I commit on the regular. I've never had someone give me the finger for spotting a quarter on the sidewalk and getting it before them. I don't actually think anyone has given me the finger for a non-valid reason face to face. In the car ... I can't count how many times it has happened. It's not like we are swimming lane to lane and in front of people. We are expending no more physical energy to drive around someone. What is *so damn offensive to people*?

Similar to the online trolls, I like to imagine the driver's next stop after waving their middle finger at me when I don't abide by their wishes. Where do they go after using their adrenaline rage to push the gas and speed away? I usually imagine they're off to the dry cleaners. They park and walk in enraged then cordially gather their freshly pressed tweed suits (extra starch) and head home for a pot roast dinner and episode of *The Brady Bunch* to cool off.

A statistic I just made up is that road rage has increased fifty-four percent in the last three years due to our political climate. Maybe it has. Maybe it hasn't. But what is at the root of anger behind the wheel and our screens? The most offensive and aggressive offender of road rage is my loving wife. I've witnessed her pick up birds with broken wings and nurse them back to health as I stand by disgusted. I've seen her tear up at the cuteness of our dogs curled up sleeping on one another. But cut her off or drive under the speed limit, and she will wish immediate death upon you. Every single time we enter a vehicle together, I wonder if we will exit still on speaking terms. "I need therapy," she will say daily in reference to her anger on the road. While I want to help her, offer her some sage advice, tell her it's okay and I support her in her time of struggle, I can't and won't. Because I just genuinely don't understand what is so awful about the road. Isn't it better and faster no matter what the "incompetent asshole" (her words not mine) in front of you is doing than a horse and buggy situation?

It's because it's not about the two mph, or the merging, or the comment someone made on Twitter that you don't agree with. It's that small part of us that we can't express anywhere else. "I become a different person behind the wheel," I'll hear. No, you don't, because any way we act, even if it's behind a screen or the wheel, is part of who we are, like it or not. It might just be one percent of our one hundred-percent makeup, but it's still the one percent we are choosing to express. It's the version you might not like, and you know no one else in your life would like it either, so it's reserved for when you are "alone." Either way—stop it. You're acting like a cnt.

CATS VS. KITTENS

After a few months in Portland, I was quickly learning that you can be whomever you want here. Riding around on a unicycle in your underwear in December is as commonplace as a defeated expression on a Monday morning. I hail from the Midwest, where if I didn't refer to pants as "slacks," it would be unclear whether I was doing life right. So, an adjustment period was needed for my new town where the city's slogan is "Keep Portland Weird." I didn't really know what this meant until one particular day.

Back in Kansas, I worked in a coffee shop. Since moving, I had been on the hunt for the perfect spot to caffeinate myself, and after around two weeks, I stumbled upon just the place. I would walk in and immediately feel like a hand-knit Afghan blanket was being wrapped around my shoulders. The cafe was lit warmly by lamps and slightly crowded with old reclaimed couches, Victorian style chairs, and walls covered with paintings the owner made herself. I felt like I was a kid walking into the "other living room" of a very fancy house. The living room with the best couches that no one sat in unless someone died, and the family was sitting Shivah. One rainy morning, I found an open couch in a corner right up against a window—the most comfortable spot in the place. I sat down with my coffee, hugged my feet up to my chest, cracked a book, and settled into what was shaping up to be a perfect Sunday afternoon.

My attention keeps for about a paragraph at a time before I have to look around, take a sip of something, or stretch my arms. I looked up and out the window at all the dogs passing by wearing raincoats more expensive than any article of clothing I owned. When I looked back down at my book for another paragraph, I was distracted by the feeling of a man staring at me. I peeked up, and our eyes met. We shared an awkward smile. There is a fine line between the amount of eye contact that warrants further action and the amount that is simply cordial, and you can feel good about resuming what you were doing before it ever happened. I quickly looked back down at my book, ensuring the latter, and, with any luck, my solitude for the duration of the morning.

An hour or so passed, and soon, I had to use the bathroom. I looked at the path I would take to get there, and right in the middle of it was Eye Contact Man. I would have to walk right past his table. The thought kept me firmly in my seat—I'd rather wet myself before talking to strangers.

Eventually, I noticed he started to pack his things. A decision needed to be made. Did I wait for him to leave or make a beeline for the bathroom while his back was turned? I stalled too long. Before I knew it, rather than happily watching him leave, I met his eyes in disbelief as he walked right over and sat next to me on the couch without my permission. Uninvited behavior like this is on par with a person feeling inclined to acknowledge having seen someone they know in the grocery store. (Always just keep walking.)

So there I sat next to a complete stranger, my entire body clenched like a butthole when you can't find a bathroom. It was hard to tell this man's age. His face lacked wrinkles, suggesting he was maybe in his thirties, but his hair and dress suggested possibly mid-fifties. He wore a wool button up shirt, the top button undone, revealing an undershirt that was perhaps white at one time. Over this he sported a thick wool vest. His hair was blonde, and he accented his receding hairline by keeping it parted to the side, creating a large V on his forehead. The couch was so old that the springs gave way as he sat, collapsing slightly in the middle until our legs touched, stopping a further fall. My knee felt hot in the worst possible way where it touched his corduroy-pant-covered leg. Unable to move, fearing more of me would cave into him, I sat rigid and motionless. He, apparently unaware of human body language, did not sense my discomfort and proceeded with his mission. He handed me a small card, an invitation of sorts, and I finally looked him in the face.

He nodded toward the card. "It's a snuggle party," he said in the same way I might say I was having a barbeque on Friday, and he should come if he was free.

All I could muster was, "Oh."

Mistaking my response for interest, he continued. "Yeah, so a group of us get together, and the point is to just, you know ... snuggle ... hold one another ..."

I didn't know. *What the fuck is a snuggle party?* An image of naked people wrapped in one another's arms forced itself into my brain. If I couldn't touch clothed knees with a stranger in a public place, I surely wouldn't fare well at this party. Just the thought made me nearly sick. But, despite my lack of response, he continued.

"Some people get really into it, and we have these huge cuddle piles. Other people are a little more timid. We call them the kittens. Typically, we have two sides of the room. The cats and the kittens." He continued without waiting for me to contribute or attempting to note my lack of interest. "The cats are really into it, and the kittens are typically newbies. But you know, it's weird ... What are those chemicals called that you get after you exercise?" he asked as he stared at the ceiling, biting his bottom lip, trying to find the word.

"Endorphins?" I contributed.

"Yeah! I leave with those! I just feel so good after." He smiled so genuinely I saw all his gums and the muffin between his teeth.

I looked down at the card with this snuggle party information typed on it. I was unable to shake the image of heavily breathing, hairy men holding me.

He kept going. "Yeah, so this is invitation only. We don't want just anyone coming, you know?"

No, I didn't know. *I'm sorry, sir, you don't want just anyone coming to your cat vs. kitten cuddle nightmare? What could the criteria possibly be? What body language did I project that made me a recipient?*

He looked at me with a steady gaze, clearly trying to read me for the first time that morning. "I'm not sure what you're thinking now."

I was thinking he was absolutely, without a doubt, the craziest motherfucker I had ever met. But I was also wondering, *What actually happens at these parties?* Did people come over and just literally lay about the floor in piles with one another? Did the host provide a spread of futon mattresses all about the house to lay upon? Did people just find a bedroom and start a pile? What if someone went to start a pile, and no one joined them, and they just lay there by themselves kind of like a messed up adult version of not being picked at recess for kickball? Or maybe a snuggle party was code for sex party because, in my head, you can't really just say, "Hey, wanna come to my sex party?" That would sound weird. But likely, if someone agreed to a snuggle party, they might also be the type of person who, once at the party, would be *down*. Right? I don't know! Because I would *never* go to a snuggle party. Hell, I would never go to a movie-watching party if I didn't know everyone there and exactly what time I could leave and go to bed. So I sat there, mildly wondering these things but making a mental note to really ponder on them later when this weirdo wasn't staring at me.

My favorite part of the entire interaction came at the very end, when he took the business card from my hand, telling me it was his last one. In its place he handed me a duplicate, a ripped off piece of paper, on which he had pre-scribbled all the information that was typed on the original card. Not worthy of the real invitation served as one of about 1,284 reasons I would not be attending.

I sat contemplating for a split second if I was a bad transplant to the city: Was I "Keeping Portland Too Normal"? In the moment, I decided no. But now, having been in Portland eleven-plus years, I wonder. I would still never go to anything remotely close to a snuggle party. But does that make that dude weird, or me? Is there even a right answer to that? Now, instead of wondering what happens at a party like that, I'm more interested in what drives a person to *go to* a party like that, regardless of what activities take place once there. Now that I am eleven years removed from that day, I actually believe it would be people not all that different from me who might go to that party, people who are afraid of random human encounters, who want a controlled environment with a knowledge of what exactly will happen when at the event. People who need some intimacy in their lives but are afraid to seek it out in a daily way. Perhaps it's the introverts of the world at snuggle parties because they are lonely. Because, for once, they want the introverted brain to not always have the last say—that they're sick of the who, what, when, where, and why being so damn important. Maybe that's just me. I don't know. But I would be remiss to not admit that a part of me wishes I went that night (even though I would still never). But there I was, fully clothed in a coffee shop and mildly freaking out because I was caving slightly into a stranger's body due to the weight of too many butts on the couch before ours.

I thanked him for the invite and sent him on his way. By that I mean I stood up, sending him bouncing to the other side of the couch, and finally went to the bathroom, the only way, at that point, I saw myself experiencing any sort of relief that morning.

CRACKS

The first week of my sophomore year of college, I met a boy named Dan on the bus back to my apartment in Lawrence, Kansas. I sat with a 1990s Caboodle in my lap, which held my art supplies. I would learn later that this very Caboodle was what piqued Dan's interest in me. In Kansas, this reason for attraction—a Caboodle and not a huge set of boobs or a face full of makeup—meant I might have met someone a little different than your average Kansas boy. An average Kansas boy would exclusively wear Jayhawk (the school's mascot) muscle tees and use Jayhawk posters for wallpaper in every room of his dark and dank apartment. If I was really lucky, Dan might even have a shoulder girdle proportionate to the size of his lower body. After all, a boy like this would know it is not always chest and back day at the gym.

I noticed Dan eyeing the art supplies and, without making eye contact, I got off the bus and started walking toward my building. My mother's warning not to talk to strangers was drilled into my head as a child and it bled into my adult life as my introverted mantra. I reconciled with myself that because mine was a large apartment complex, this boy would surely be gone before I made it to the building, but as I approached the building, a hand extended in front of me and opened the door.

"Hi, I'm Dan. Are those art supplies?"

Unsure how to proceed, I stepped inside. "Yes, I'm an art major."

"I take it you live in this building?" He pointed to the first door on the left. "I'm this apartment right here. What's your name?"

"I'm Melissa," I said, adding, "Well, I guess we are upstairs neighbors then." I lived in the place directly above him.

Walking toward his door, he called back, "Well, I'll see you around, Melissa," and he disappeared into his apartment.

I trudged upstairs in my end-of-the-day stupor, thinking about that short interaction with Dan. He was surprisingly cute. To this point in college, I had managed to attract mostly frat boys while we lingered in a blissful state of a Natty Lite buzz, causing each of us to find the other attractive *enough*. I had slept with none of them but had I partaken, it would have warranted no award to me, as they would sleep with a cardboard cutout of a woman if it meant another notch on their disgusting bunk beds.

The next morning, Caboodle in tow, I walked outside my apartment half hoping I might see Dan at the bus stop and mostly hoping I wouldn't see him ever again. As I walked out the door, a note fell at my feet. *"It was nice meeting you on the bus - Dan."* His phone number was scribbled underneath in scribe that made me wonder if he had a six-year-old child. I stood looking at the note, wondering if it was some practical joke. I could not believe a girl carrying a Caboodle would have left a cute, normal-seeming boy thinking about her the next morning. Dan was the epitome of surfer meets rock climber in both appearance and dress. That day on the bus, he had on a tie-dyed shirt and loose-fitting pants that one might leisurely wear from a capoeira class to spinning poi outside in the quad. While I was not ugly, I had the typical self-esteem an eighteen-year-old girl might. In my youth, I sported braces for eighty years, a very short haircut that was described as "cuuuute" by adults in my life with a bit too much emphasis on the "uuuu," implying it was all lies, and, as mentioned, I possessed a very muscular, if not oddly masculine, build. While the hair had grown, the braces had closed in the inch gaps between all my teeth, and boobs had formed (defying all odds), I still walked the world as if I were forever that awkward twelve-year-old, constantly surprised and suspicious should anyone treat me differently.

Low self-esteem usually put me in a place where, should a guy express interest, I wouldn't question if I reciprocated it. I only burdened myself with the task of convincing him to continue to *like* like me, treating the whole affair as though one minor misstep would cue him in to the dork I really was, and it would all be over. So, naturally, I called Dan.

A few weeks and a couple of dates later, we were sitting in the stairwell of our apartment building. There was a window at the top of the stairs that ran from floor to ceiling. It was always covered in water marks, surely never windexed, but keeping with the atmosphere of the rest of the complex, occupied mostly by dirty college students. Around three p.m., the sun shone directly through the window, blinding passersby to the fact that it wasn't clean. Light bounced off all the walls into the tiny stairwell, illuminating the whole place. Dan and I would lean against the window or sit on the top step with the sun in our faces talking about our life plans. These moments felt like clean sheets. Like we weren't in a dingy building that might fall if the wind was too strong. Like we were treating ourselves to a fleeting moment that we might not believe we deserved.

Dan would be described by most in Kansas as someone who marched to the beat of a different drum. I have found that this is more a descriptor for people relative to their location. Dan was a rare breed for Kansas; now that I'm a resident of Portland, he would seem just like another raindrop on the sidewalk. I liked him because he was genuinely interested in people's lives and their stories. "How are you?" would not be flippant from his mouth. He would want to know but "How *are* you" while looking into your eyes. I've always been wary of extreme eye contact makers. *What are they looking for?* And usually,

Why are they standing so close to me? They seem interested but somehow blissfully unaware of your backward steps away from their close-talking eye contact as they generally match each step you take back with two steps forward.

While we sat there one afternoon in our illuminated sanctuary, he asked me a question, therapist style, while leaning with his back against the wall, chin resting on his hands that were placed over one bent knee.

"What are your cracks in life?"

Insert extreme eye contact.

"What do you mean by 'cracks'?" I asked, shifty eyed, looking at everything but him. At this point in my life, the number of deep conversations I'd had were few and pretty much all with Dan. I didn't have an answer for him because I hadn't been forced to think about it. I grew up in the land of midwestern suburbia where most people tucked their issues safely beyond their white picket fences, past their large manicured lawns, and behind their oversized, tightly closed front doors with the large brass knocker that was double-lock-bolted shut, ironically so because bets are pretty damn safe that whatever lurked indoors was way scarier than anything roaming the streets of Fill in the Blank Estates. We didn't talk about our problems back home. We folded them up neatly like the clean linens we kept on hand in case an important guest might stay over, then we stored them until arrival so far back in the closet that we forgot they existed at all. So when a cute blonde-haired boy who had clearly been raised to *communicate* stared at me in a sunlit stairwell and asked me about my life, I had nothing for him. I wanted to take the clean sheets I felt like I was finally slipping into and walk out into the sunlight and air them out, shaking them until the dust all came off and wrap myself in them while sharing all my thoughts. But I didn't even understand his question. It would take years of the most tedious excavation before I would even realize something special, if not cracked, might reside within me.

"I'd have to think about that," I answered.

Our relationship blossomed as most college ones do; I feigned interest in football and pretended to want to learn the rules, and Dan happily taught me in between bouts of yelling at the TV. Too poor to go out to dinner, we would sometimes go to the college rec center and climb on the bouldering wall or lift weights then go back to his apartment and make popcorn or heat up something frozen for dinner. He could bounce effortlessly from typical football-loving college dude to *I'm sorry, what the fuck did you just say, Mr. Hippie?* in like a second.

"Yeah, so I'm trying this energy stuff," he told me one night after one particularly heated Chiefs ball game.

"You're trying what now?" I said, looking up from the nutrition label on the Hot Pockets, trying to determine if any of the ingredients were food.

"It's like, I want to be able to stare at something, like that Hot Pocket box, and will it to move with my *mind.* You know what I mean? Like it would move over to me but neither of us would be touching it."

"I see. That sounds cool. You should keep practicing," I said supportively as I moved the Hot Pocket to the microwave with my actual hands.

Dan and I dated for a year on and off. For me, the end of relationships with men was never sad. It always felt more like what I imagine being liberated from entrapment under a pickup truck might feel like. One minute, I'm being crushed and dying, and the next, I'm totally free and have been given the gift of life by some nice passerby who found the adrenaline induced strength to lift a truck off my nearly dead body and set me free. I don't remember the exact conversation when Dan and I decided we would be just friends. What I remember is that we had the conversation in his bedroom, and after we walked out into his living room, he turned to me. "Want to watch an episode of *Family Guy?*"

"I really do," I said jumping onto his couch. Now that we weren't a couple, I felt like I had finally come clean about a secret or like I had a *checked everything off my to-do list before the weekend was over* kind of feeling.

"Great, I'll go get some popcorn."

And we watched a few hours of *Family Guy,* interspersed with looking at each other and cracking up as we raised the volume to try and drown out the screams of his roommate having sex in the next room. God, I miss college.

I remember looking at Dave that night and thinking, *He's awesome.*

Soon, the feeling of freedom would wear off after a breakup. It always did. I would leave one prison for another: be with someone I'm not interested in vs. be with myself, whom I didn't understand. A constant dance between which feeling I could escape from next. The in-between time always feeling euphoric, like that initial high that never lasts. And I would begin the search again.

The primary commonality that I saw among every man I dated was that I didn't want to be around them all that much. I couldn't see that perhaps the actual common denominator in the equation was me. I would even let them know I could not commit to hanging out more than twice a week, tops. I would actually tell them this. It was in the verbal manual they got upon hanging out with me for two weeks or more—Chapter 1: This Too Shall Pass.

I would often muse to my friends, "I should date someone who doesn't live in the same city. How amazing would that be? We could just see each other on the weekends, and I could do whatever I want on weekdays."

Years later, after college and the days of Dan, I dated a man named John. The two relationships were similar in that we were more friends than a couple, and we would break up every few months or so then get back together again, usually due to a mutual liking of recreational activities. One night, John and I were walking back to our cars together after being out at a bar. We had driven separately, as both of us had come from work, and as we walked toward our cars, I was silently racking my brain for a reason to go home alone, an excuse to not need a visitor in my bed. *My roommate is sick; my mom is sad, and I should call her; I should really floss*—all reasonable excuses to head home; I just needed to pick one and stick to my story. My car was parked across the street from his van, and without pausing, I muffled an "Okay, bye" as I gave him a quick side hug and got into my car. I thought inside, *I could just drive away. I could just go home and go to sleep by myself.* With a deep breath, the thought even calmed me. But not hearing his engine start, I knew I had to roll down my window.

"Do you want to come over?" he asked as any person would ask their partner after a night out.

I stalled, not saying anything. He sat there, one arm out his window, the other on his steering wheel. He looked at me from across the street, not seeing my leg rapidly bouncing up and down as I sat in my car, blanketed in the safety of its steel frame, in nervous contemplation. Finally, I said, "I'm pretty tired. I think I'm just going to head home." I felt terrible. I didn't feel terrible because he didn't get what he wanted but because I had no real explanation as to why I didn't want the same thing. That night in particular, I felt like something was wrong with me. John checked all the boxes: I had fun with him, he was really nice, we laughed, we had similar interests, we didn't like kids, we did like vans and shitty beer and burritos. What was the fucking problem? I couldn't put my finger on it. That night was the first time I knew something more than "I'm just not interested in that guy" was happening, but my brain wasn't letting me in on what I was feeling. It felt like an itch in the very center of my back that I couldn't get to alone but was pushing away everyone who wanted to help.

I texted John a few months into our third go at dating: *"Let's grab a coffee and talk tomorrow morning if you're free."* We sat in the corner at our favorite coffee shop. John would always buy a baked item, and I would only order coffee. One hundred percent of the time, I would eat at least half of whatever he got. That day, I wondered if I should've bought my own. I didn't.

We sat mute, facing each other. Not generally the one to instigate plans or hesitate in taking a bite of his pastry, I'm sure he knew something was amiss. *Maybe I should excuse myself to the bathroom and text him what I wanted to talk about from there. While he's reading the text, I could slip out the front door and be on my way to Canada.*

We sat there in an awkward silence, and after a few minutes, I finally felt okay enough to dig in on my half of his pastry. The words I wanted to say felt like vomit as they traveled up my throat, only to be swallowed back down. So I made small talk.

"How's work?"

"Work is the same ..." he responded with a tone that implied he knew something was up and wondered why I didn't just spit it out.

After an intolerable amount of time and internal self-talk, I decided to say what I came to say. What came out was poetic—the most beautiful words worthy of being stitched on a pillow or printed on a poster for others to quote and use at their will.

"I don't think I'm that into dudes."

"Oh," he said, looking genuinely confused as he should have been. After a silence, "So, does this mean we're breaking up?"

"Um, I think it does," I said, fighting back tears and longing for the historically light-and-free feeling that I associated with breakups.

We left the coffee shop and exchanged an odd but necessary hug, which lingered a length of time that implied support.

The next few days felt like I was mourning a death, but no one had actually died, so I just ended up feeling self-involved, even narcissistic for feeling this great loss that really only affected me. People were killed for being gay, lost their jobs, kids, places to live. People lost so much more than I was losing or more than I was aware I was losing at the time. I was living in a very liberal city, I had friends who accepted everyone, my family probably, maybe, wouldn't care. But still, this grief and embarrassment for not even knowing this *thing* about myself came over me, and I couldn't do much but cry. Someone had died—the old me. The person I thought I was and tried to be for so long was gone, and now I had to start over. And that was fucking scary.

For me, the phrase "coming out" has never felt right because, for me, it was more a coming together of memories and experiences, which all shared that feeling I couldn't put my finger on, like looking at John in his van and wondering what was wrong with me for not wanting to go home with him. Now, looking at that patchwork quilt of experiences, I can piece together what it all meant. You see, "coming out" always implies a knowledge a person had of themselves previously that they weren't sharing with the rest of the world. That's why it doesn't feel like it applies to me. I was not sharing that knowledge with myself. But then suddenly, out of nowhere, I felt like I deserved that feeling of slipping between crisp, clean, fresh sheets. Because I finally let myself in, and being let in on a secret you've been keeping from yourself is a lot like discovering what the cracks are in your life and closing them in one at a time until you feel whole.

Thank you for reading
Cracks:
Unapologetic Essays on Growing Up and Getting Gay
If you enjoyed this book, please leave an online review.

CONNECT WITH MELISSA SHER
Website: melissa-sher.com
Instagram: sher.melissa
Facebook: facebook.com/melissa.sher.56

95764540R00079